Timely Issues

GE

Also by Elizabeth Jennings

Selected Poems
Collected Poems
Times and Seasons
Familiar Spirits
A Poet's Choice
In the Meantime
Praises

ELIZABETH JENNINGS

Timely Issues

CARCANET

Published in Great Britain in 2001 by
Carcanet Press Limited
4th Floor, Conavon Court
12–16 Blackfriars Street
Manchester M3 5BQ

A CIP catalogue record for this book
is available from the British Library

ISBN 1 85754 515 X

The publisher acknowledges financial assistance
from the Arts Council of England

Set in Monotype Garamond by XL Publishing Services, Tiverton
Printed and bound in England by SRP Ltd, Exeter

For Dr Hywel W. Jones

Contents

Regions of Memory   9
A Company of Friends   10
Dance   11
Mozart in the Middle of the Night   12
Dream: A Ballad   13
The Story   14
Country Sounds   15
Out in the Country in 2000   16
Caring   17
Well-Being   18
Vigour   19
Lullaby for the Old   20
Rage of the Moon   21
October 2000   22
The Thinker   23
For Any Newish Poet   24
Prayer: Homage to George Herbert   25
Homage to Thomas Traherne   26
Homage to Gerard Manley Hopkins:
    After Receiving Communion in Hospital   27
Homage to Robert Graves   28
Reflection   29
Looking at Pictures   30
I Concerning Imagination   31
II Concerning Imagination   32
III Concerning Imagination   33
Diagnosis   34
An Awareness   35
Some Months After Anaesthetics   36
Tenderness   37
Lost Time   38
After Four Months of Illness   39
One More Place of Memory   40
Assurance   41
Advice   42
The Hours   43
Prophets   44

Girl at Prayer   45
Advent   46
At Mass   47
All Saints 2000   48
All Souls   49
Song in November 2000   50
Carol for 2000   52
New Year Song   53
Epiphany 2001   54
Night Song   55
Whitsun   56
Hope   57
Eden   58
Perfection   59
Assurance Beyond Midnight   60

Regions of Memory

(After an Operation)

Regions of memory – I returned from these
Not with a map but with a hard-learned awe.
I know the spirit's travails and its peace,
Have found there is no law

To help you through the trees and gardens of
Memory. All life is different where
The mind is moved by hidden brooks of love,
Forests of kindness, almost a sacred air.
You cannot find in books

Useful guides to paths where memory
Treads softly. I have come back to a place
Of argument and discord but can see
Skies of sifted gold, a silver space
Where everyone is free.

Regions of memory – when you've been there
For long you're changed. Those regions teach you how
To deal with enemies like dark and fear;
And how to praise. Here. Now.

A Company of Friends

We were all friends that night and sitting round
A lateish dinner. Candles lit us and
Shyness disappeared. Some golden ground
Surely held us. We could understand
Love's mishaps, teenage children and the sound
    Of their troubles. Here,

Close to a river and a city where
Learning's been current long, you could accept
Its implications. Last night we could share
The worth of art and promises well kept
Until that hour. Here was a world of care
    And I think we all slept

Better for our words of joy and grief.
We ate, we drank, ideas seemed to come
So easily. Here was abundant life
And grace shone like a happy coming home.
We did not notice that the time was brief
    As every candle flame.

We gave time back to one another as
We shook warm hands and called a clear Good Night.
Now it's last night's tomorrow and I pass
That feast like film before my eyes and light
My long room with that silver and that glass
    And glory in the sight.

Dance

Always at the heart of things there is dance,
    Dances of death, dances of angels where
Christ is there is always a dance of Rising
    For saving is always a dance that takes our hands,

Tells us the joy of endurance, the steps of pain.
    Prayer is the deepest dance and it can be
Stately and homely, high, serene and sweet.
    Where there is love that's hurt there is also dance,
And Creation is a dance, a constant movement.
    The stars dance in their high places, the moon
Dances and alternates with every sunset
    And with every sunrise too.

Mozart in the Middle of the Night

In the still night the cool notes fall,
Mozart elaborates the silence as
Note after note seem to be hanging, then
He lets them fall as if into a pool.
My lamp is shining. Gold is everywhere.
Ah, now the drops are gold. They disappear
One after the other, one again, and yet
Again another. They are caught now in a net.
Alfred Brendel can control them all
And yet 'control' is not the proper word.
In the night there is a singing sun.
I listen in a rapture of repose;
Drop after drop, there another goes.

Dream: A Ballad

It was no dream and yet it was not waking,
A story told itself within my mind
But it went further; there was bright day-breaking
And huntsmen hungry for the lucky find.

Was I the centre? No. So much occupied
Within my seeing and, much further on,
I heard the grateful and auspicious word,
Saw the broad opening of the morning sun.

World upon world. I was not well indeed
And yet what I have gathered from it all!
Dancers making music showed their need
And there was neither apple nor a fall.

The Story

I knew that it lay about me,
I knew that the story I had to live was near
But fenced off. Only I
Could find the entrance, and not by straining and fighting
But only, always by

Being prepared for the great surrender, the huge
Advance and appearance. Nothing to do with fear
Was this. I only had
To let the four seasons march in order ahead,
To watch the sky changing and meeting the sea.
This was the way I had to let things happen,
To let the world appear
In all its golden finish and lucky end.
I watched the door of morning start to open,
I simply put out my hand.

Country Sounds

We really lived in the country,
In the long school summer holidays we shouldered
Our way through a thin wooden fence straight to a field
Where the hay was high and sweet-smelling, the sun crisped it and
There were poppies and shepherd's purse and cow-parsley
And the smell of grass and the buzz and murmur of insects.
Our home was big and near enough to the city,
A beautiful university but we,
My sister and I, basked and flourished in green.
Deft with her hands always she would build
Small hay igloos. We'd sit in the dark smell
And plan an easy war with bows and arrows.
No one actually suffering of course.
For we were in a mood shaped by the huge sun
Bowling overhead.
And we were in a trance of murmurous summer sounds
Its music sighing and blowing,
And we learnt much all the time
Whole histories of how things thrive and spread
And we packed our imaginations with country lore
Dreams of milking and taking in the harvest.

Today this cannot be.
That field and every approach to it is built on
With houses of different designs, all showing cars.
And so our country life is a memory,
A mood and a music too.
Our counterparts today don't own a field,
Can't share our languid pleasure.
        I wish I could
Offer our pleasant field to them and let
Them learn the wisdom of every summer sound.

Out in the Country in 2000

I shall not forget this summer
With all its moods of water and of light,
With all its hasty sky and tunnelled roads.
I shan't forget so many
Greens beyond green, the sage, the weed, the mournful
Evergreens. There've been such raids of light
Down side-roads which we drove down, through the neat
Important, tugging river.

I shan't forget the sound
Of many birds excited by the breeze,
On hunting trips, the young out testing wings
And tumbling with the clouds
All this through side-roads, lanes of Oxfordshire
And Warwickshire, so ripe and clean and busy.

I took new vigour from the rush of winds
I drank the light and felt it in my veins.
I praise the countryside that's still to find,
Waiting so patiently,
Giving, oddly, such strong peace of mind.

Caring

It was all scientific to start with,
The voice, male, young, not excited,
Not at first, that is.
But the radio voice became much warmer, much keener,
And the subject, *Life Before Birth*, became important.
The young obstetrician didn't hide what he felt
And the woman whose labour only lasted two hours
Kept saying 'It hurt very badly, you've no idea',
But the doctor *had* an idea, His voice revealed it,
The words came faster as, with enormous pride,
Which I could accept at once,
He said 'A baby is much, much tougher than we are,
Before it is born, I mean.
For example, our brains won't survive more than three minutes
Without any oxygen,
But an unborn child can do without it much longer
It has to be tough, you see, for its long, dark journey.
So full of hazards and dangers.'
He went on talking and I
Found quite suddenly I was close to tears.
Why? Why? Why?
I think now because so much care was present
So much compassion, almost all of it practical.
Life Before Birth is an almost epic subject,
So many hardships and obstacles,
So much longing to live.
The young doctor's voice paused sometimes and I
Realized how carried away he was by his subject,
How much he wanted premature lives to continue
How far away from anything that must die.
How rapid the hands I could not see must have looked,
How eloquent his eye.

Well-Being

I savour it as it returns to me,
    This health, this flow along
My bones and veins, this wholesome energy
Which can create rich thoughts or drifts of song.

Any poison halts the inward flow;
    Illness takes away
The strength of love almost. Art seems to go
Relentlessly. There is more night than day.

Now I am glad and grateful and relearn
    The taste of happiness.
My thoughts with almost tenderness now turn
To making poems, creation's hopefulness.

Vigour

Sometimes each day proclaims itself as if
    I had not seen it so
Before. It has such glow, such sheen, such life.
The oldest flowers seem freshly now to grow,

And every sky I gaze at shows a sun
    Of huge power and extent.
From being ill I'm well and I've begun
My life afresh. I understand what's meant.

New ideas are spoken. I am full
    Of longing now to know
How creation shows such fulsome skill,
How all the winds seem fertile when they blow.

I see before I understand and then
    Interpret and explore.
I move in joy around this world of men
And beg more life, more freshness, more and more.

Celebration falling like kind rain
New skies that have new planets in their store.

Lullaby for the Old

The old need a lullaby
    As much as the young.
I think of right words to sigh
    Into a song.

A song that reminds of the past
    And all of its joys.
May all through the night my song last
    Sounding 'Rejoice'.

Rage of the Moon

Rest, heavy head, on the wood
    Of the good, old desk-stand.
Dreams must be understood
    And the right hand

Feels for purchase upon
    A fine, old, open page
Of writing lit by the moon
    And its light rage.

October 2000

The leaves hang tardily. There's been such rain
And now today the sky is wide and clear
Of all but radiant clouds. After huge rain
We are amazed at the dry atmosphere

And potent sun that glitters through pale blue
And tender puffs of cloud. Rain disappeared,
Summer has not quite gone. What it can do
Now that the land's been winnowed and is clear –

Imagination gathers insights now,
A slightly teasing landscape keeps alert
Leaf after leaf, still green on twig and bough.
Here is a country for the hopeful heart.

The Thinker

He is mild-mannered and some people say
'He's in another world.' They are quite wrong,
He is in now and here, and every day
He thinks of plans to which we all belong.

He's read past notions. In his mind he holds
A shape, a purpose, meaning written live.
Night and day he watches now our world's
Behaving wildly. He wants it to thrive.

He wants all men to share his appetite
For truth. It is a way of life, a choice
Of how to be and know. He claims no right
But tries to be a civilized, true voice.

For Any Newish Poet

There is this habit now of nonchalance –
One writes of death but doesn't use the word.
They might allow the words 'a dance of death'
    Or something overheard.

There is this habit of concealing art:
You do not say you fear and let alone
Love anyone. You have, of course, a heart
    But now it is not done

To say you care. O yes but English verse
Comes echoing back: 'I am behind the art
I am the feeling when you love to curse,
    I am the vital part

Of everything you write.' Remember Yeats,
Don't forget Auden's perfect adjective
So unexpected. English poetry waits
    Always for you to give

What feels like novelty. The new is so
Resistant. Never mind. Dare to allow
The word that leaps to mind. O let it grow
    And be part of your now.

Prayer: Homage to George Herbert

George Herbert said it all. All I can do
Is show my hesitancies now and try
To fit my different, later words into
Another way to say Our Lord will die.

He hangs upon the Cross and I seek words
And how they can be lifted into prayer.
The soldiers come with hammers and with swords
And flies are buzzing in the blinding air.

Shall I seek opposites as Herbert did
To reach the truth? I need the spirit to
Leap through flesh. Language must be rid

Of all half-meanings. Christ needs words to show
He's dying. O indeed now he is dead
But I shall need the words that rise also.

Homage to Thomas Traherne

Your prose could hardly be more close to verse.
It soars, it sings, and God is your great theme,
Your paeans to Him never seem to cease,
He filled each waking moment and, in dream,

God surely must have faced you gladly with
All his graces shining, sweet and clear.
You never needed to have fear of death
Yet your contrition was not hard to hear.

Your *Centuries* are noble, rich, serene,
Leaping with love and dancing with delight
And it is clear exactly what you mean.

Traherne, you've lighted up my blackest night.
Your work is quick, direct, exact and keen
And everywhere I read I come on light.

Homage to Gerard Manley Hopkins:
After Receiving Communion in Hospital

Hopkins, I understand exactly now
What you meant when you told us that the sick
Endear us to them. I know this is true
Because I am a sick one and God's quick,

Saving principle has come to me,
A tiny piece of bread unleavened saves
The soul. I feel its power immediately.
Stammering my thanks, I know my flesh behaves

Oddly, but I know also I am
Within Heaven's confines. You, O Hopkins I
Commend for showing me how close I came

To our Redeemer in his healing, high
Offices. My thanksgiving is home
And Jesus Christ is with me where I lie.

Homage to Robert Graves

The lyric, that true, traditional sound
You were in touch with all your life. I owe
More debts than I can pay. I love your ground
Which blossoms into song. You did eschew

Modernism but it did not matter,
You had no need of it, you were so strong.
You tell us of fierce love. None can do better,
It makes us see death darkening every song.

'Death's food at last in his true rank and order'
You wrote and you were right. Yes, Robert Graves,
You wrote much else, stood never on a border.

You knew the moods of love, how it behaves
And you stored language like a busy hoarder.
I move about among your golden leaves.

Reflection

Wisdom comes without a sage,
    Music finds harmony
That asks for no composer of any age.
    Thus, sometimes, poetry.

Looking at Pictures

(in memory of C. V. Wedgewood)

Your presence lit the paintings for me but
Only to show more radiantly how each
Impressionist, say, in his own way caught
A slant of sun, a pool of shade. To teach

Like this is not to teach at all but fill
Another's eyes with your own way of seeing.
You let the biggest buffet go so still
That I too entered in the painter's being.

And so we walked from galleries to see
A world transformed. Thus every visit went
When you were picking paintings out for me,

Making the shortest time a large event,
Now I'm alone but you have set me free
In all art's history from those hours we spent.

I Concerning Imagination

It is at all great starts of things. Recall
The Tree, the Garden and the promise, all
Appeared in nursery tales and nursery rhymes.
Imagination furnishes all times
That show a lucid and an empty space.
There was a whisper even then of grace
And grace is what a nanny taught you long
Before you'd heard the other use of song,

How everything is swarming with odd light
When you look back to find your first goodnight.
Haven't you been searching everywhere
For places which halt time and hold you there?
Eden had its cradle – songs you knew
And Eden wasn't very long ago
When you read history and noticed how
Imagination chooses then or now.

And then the many faiths, the countless cults,
It is not your imagining which halts.
And you can't run from it for in your dreams
Images rise and joy or terror comes
How is it to be held, how fixed and framed?

It won't need orders or the cold command,
No, let it be, and, let alone, it may
Grow without you. It did yesterday,
But do not think tomorrow's at your beck
Entirely. Human will can love or wreck.
Remember all the frightening history.
Imagination is no mystery
But it can haunt whatever you may do
And can be both the ghost and haunted too.

II Concerning Imagination

It can round known galaxies, scan light
    And yet there must be rules.
It has its own bewildering stretch of light
And it can make the owners of it fools.

When it digs deep or leaps across the sky
    It is a kind of grace
Offered to almost everyone. Then why
Is it so trammelled by the human race?

In the baby crying after birth
    It is already laid
Intricately and gently in our earth.
Yet from our start we knew we have betrayed

Some unreached tenderness, some dear compassion.
    Our will plays its strong part
In the uses of imagination
Which comes the moment there's a human heart.

III Concerning Imagination

It is reality, it must be stressed,
     And not its opposite.
We place its aura over everything
     By our power make it fit
A tiny mood, great art, a way to sing,
     It's more than to exist.

Wallace Stevens made each poem he wrote
     Show differences between
Imagination and reality.
     And yet for everyone,
By casting his own glow he showed how we
     All somehow have brought

The two together. All we imagine is
     A bonus to all things.
We heighten every exploit that we know.
     Imagining means wings
Which lift the usual, give it light, and so
     Our purpose here is this.

Diagnosis

The doctor talks. The students gather round.
I'm opposite this patient in a bed
Close enough to hear each separate sound.
I heard each syllable the doctor said
But I am carefully bound

To seeming not to listen. Doctor goes,
Students chat and smile and disappear.
That patient opposite is wrapped in fear,
She turns and pulls her sheets and blanket close.
I am so far though near.

The patient's name is Milly. Now and then
We've talked of trivial things. We've never said
A word about our illnesses. Her pain
Is obvious to me. Will she be dead
Soon? What does it mean

That operation which the doctor told
Her wasn't 'very serious'? I knew
The very opposite was what was true.
I dared not show compassion and be bold
And tell her that I knew.

At length knowing I could not find the right words
To fit the time, I kept our talks upon
Humdrum matters. She would point out cards
She had received. Her operation's soon.
O human nature's cards

Ought to be tougher and more sensitive.
The very contradiction makes me see
How far we are from powerful sympathy.
I do not know how long that friend will live
But feel her lack in me.

An Awareness

When did I first know I'd been close to death?
When did the dark, negotiating birds
Swarm away and their sounds turn to words?
When did the wide air clear and show me growth
      Was what I moved towards?

Pain released me, anaesthetics lost
Their power. People's faces became clear.
It was as if a sweet, migrating host
Turned and brought Summer back and placed me near
      Where the sun shone most.

The minute-hands were moving on most watches,
The chimes of all clocks sounded steady hours.
Lights seemed everywhere that each limb stretched
Towards when healthy. O I felt new powers
      Building me fresh beaches.

I fell in love with the tides, and love renewed,
Restored, re-made me. Life put kindly hands
Out for my need. There was not any feud
Between the ill and well but now new lands
Showed me everywhere fresh flowers, ripe food
      And I could understand.

Some Months After Anaesthetics

It is as if I'd never seen before
The block of gold that's melted in the air,
It was indeed a largesse of good ore
That's painted all the shadows everywhere.
It is as if a door

Opened in the East this morning and
Spread out richly everywhere; torched flower
From white to yellow, lighted on a hand
That settled anywhere. It is a power
In sky and on the land.

In early Spring I left my sick-bed and
Tangle of memory and gazed around.
I was enriched and altered, found a friend
In everything. This morning all the ground
Is gold that will not end.

It will only be concealed at last
When cool comes back and we turn round the sun
But I shall have no feeling of a past
Or credit that the sun has really gone.
My mind makes happy haste,

And my imagination is restored
And lively, richer than it was before
Sickness held me. Memory's now a hoard
Of rich landscapes and insights. My mind's door
Shows an unearned reward.

Tenderness

(for Alyson)

I can't remember any tenderness
Like this before. When I was weak and ill
A gentle nurse would wash me. My distress
She calmed at once. I can remember still
Each quiet move, calm word. I marvel this

Can happen for I'm independent and
Think that I am able to take care
Of myself. With her hand on my hand,
Washing was a kind of joke to share.
There's so much more today I understand
And now I owe the whole of it to her.

Lost Time

Shall I never recall those hours when I
Lay drugged beneath the nameless surgeon's knife
Or in some bed or ward? I did not die
Though I was told I nearly lost my life.
Again, again I try

To bring back memory and every mood
Which it contains. What spaces did my mind
Inhabit? What great scenes, some sad, some good
Did I discover? Was I deaf and blind
Or in some neighbourhood

Out of time that memory won't yield?
I have haphazard, pell mell scraps of thoughts,
Far views of now a road and now a field
Of grazing cows? Or was I in great courts
Of princes which conceal

Histories of hopes or wars, or both? Who can
Offer me each event that fits these hours?
I beg my friends for knowledge and they scan
Moments when they saw me with no powers
Of usual days. No man

Or woman can retrieve that land. I knew
Its dreams, its riches and its emptiness.
I know that there is nothing I can do
To bring back all that lost time. So distress
Comes because the true

Events my spirit wandered in are lost
And my present lacks some grace, some sign
And yet what wonders hit me when I crossed
The threshold back to consciousness to find
All things aglow with grace.

After Four Months of Illness

Coming out of illness, I feel shy
As if the world around were new to me,
As if, as in vexed youth, I now must try
New doors which seemed to be

Locked and bolted. I've been in a closed
World (a world of open fear sometimes)
But nurses, doctors had their cures and used
Them carefully. Old rhymes

Of poetry came back to me before
The words of mannerly discourse. I'm glad
Poetry has such a grip. I push a door
Open and feel sad

Not to hear or see great celebrations,
Simply people caught off-guard who try
Not to stare. So, with imagination's
Fresh vigour I defy

My own uncertainty but I can't be
Bold as I wish. Too much has happened and
I know that I look pale and thin. I see
A world once usual new lit up for me.
I try to understand

Why such a flood of light shines everywhere,
Except for sudden darks. All this is new,
Yet there's an invitation in the air
And I walk slowly through the pell mell glow,
Then stand quite still and stare.

So much energy went into this
Return of mine. Long convalescence can't
Prepare you fully for a genesis.
I wonder where I'll fit for O I want
To find love, happiness.

One More Place of Memory

There are mysterious places where I've been
But only keep their echoes in my mind,
Also their fragrance. I have never seen
Colours like theirs before or since. I find
It hard to tell now of this curious land
And yet it haunts me. I can't understand

Why long sickness brought me into such
Woods and clearings. I declare the sun
Which shone there was a beacon, yes a torch
Lighting the earth up. O how hard it shone
And left new coins upon the forest floor
Where I was standing. I would say much more

But no words catch the glowings that I knew
Within that space where no clock ticked and where
Colours outshone the rainbow. Very few
People brushed past me but I did not care,
And yet I wish I had a map, a chart
To point out all I learnt. I need new art,

To show, as Baudelaire did, we too can
Mingle the senses. Yes, that comes most near
What I experienced. I indeed learnt then
A radiance that I could almost hear,
Sights I could touch. Maybe later on
I'll find the cadences which halt that sun.

Assurance

My love, I hold you in imagination,
    Either mine or yours
And it is stronger than remembered passion.
It uses memory with all its force.

O and the clocks go silent, time departs,
    Now is forever here.
How delicate yet strong are our two hearts,
Mine beats for you now almost everywhere.

Only when my world is rent with storm,
    Threatened by sadness or
Overcome by black words which can come
And threaten me with the inner, hideous war,

Only then, I've lost you, O but fast
    A little flash of sun,
A hurrying memory returns you blessed
And our great love is stalwartly at one.

Advice

Best to be still and meditate
And let the broken heart alone.
There is a pure and timely state
That reaches through both flesh and bone.
    O yes be still and gently wait
And neither trade nor own.

There is a quiet state of mind
Where images can dance until
Their own true landscape they can find
And where the heart is one with will
    In this way harvesting can bind
And nights are always still.

Wait, do not justify or trade
Or make excuses. What you need
Is something you have never made
And never understood indeed.
    Thus mind and heart are both obeyed
And to fruition lead.

The Hours

Out of silence they come, out of their own
Eloquent silences they join together
Into the wide church they come as the bells
Start the beginning of Hours, the singing of Hours.
These are silent men who come together
Out of their secret prayers into the open,
The cool and open, undecorated space
Of their wide church. Day after day and night
After night throughout the months and every year,
Monks sing the same words, save for the special ones,
The rich, enlarging Hours of the great Feasts,
Christmas and Easter and the darker Hours,
The penitential ones of open prayer,
Prayer that pierces the sun and rounds the moon,
Moves through the trees and over the roofs of houses.
The Hours are eternal in their repetitions,
The monks die and others take their places,
Young men who give up everything for the rich
Eloquence of prayer and the words of God,
God as Man and spirit and Three in One.
Hours sing the praises of the sacred Three
And the daily Masses, the bread turned into flesh
And wine to Blood, the Hours Hosanna and say
All that need be said in the singing voice.
Listen, the night is passing, the *Gloria*
Praises the dawn, the Lamb of God is sung
Into the rising sun and day appearing.
Hour after Hour, they will proceed forever,
Telling our Birth and sanctifying death,
Tolling and ringing, bringing the great good news
And the saving of souls and all the contrition of men.

Prophets

Into our history great prophets break
And they halt time with what they have to say.
Even sceptics want to hear them speak
Perhaps to catch them out and so betray.
They're cynics. Many make

Sounds of praise and wonder. Prophets give
Shape to our lives and touch our purposes.
They draw up rules and laws to help us live
With pride. They'll pause distress,

Comfort the grieving, make the happy more
Content. Great prophets are forerunners of
God and bear his early words. We are
Excited when we hear them speak of love.
We welcome every seer.

It is as if there is some need in us,
Isaiah, John the Baptist can fulfil.
They surely always have the power to bless
Our little plans. At best, they make us still
And alter us with grace.

Girl at Prayer

The girl simply raises her hand
And salutes the sudden sun and blesses it.
She is learning the lesson of love,
And trying to understand
That she need not search for words
Or make many movements either.
All she need do is copy the sun's behaviour
Or the moon's silent entry at night.

Advent

Comings gather here to celebrate.
Almost impossible adventures now
Take place and all excessive dreams can meet
And no one even wants to question why
Bright lights assume a street,

Stars stand in order. One or two may fall,
We are awestruck, full of gratitude.
Marvels can happen, we invite them all
Into a sudden state of wanting good.
Yes now every tall

Story comes true. A child is on his way,
Unborn as yet but carried in the womb
Of a virgin. She chose to agree
To this. O all the world makes ample room
For everyone to be

Enchanted in a state of graciousness
Not all choose well but possibilities
Blossom about us. In the Christmas Trees
Waiting around we watch our happiness
And some fall to their knees.

At Mass

It is the order which we know so well,
The 'alleluija' here, the 'Amen' there
That concentrates the awe, makes drama fill
Whatever shape the church is. We can hear
Jerusalem is there,

Or maybe it is Bethlehem indeed.
People rise and genuflect, then bow
Their heads and by the gesture intercede.
The Mass proceeds and this is always how
We show how vast a need

Is satisfied. The Elevation is
Rushing by the bell and yet hours hesitate,
Time withdraws while human ecstasies
Take on the power in which we contemplate
How Mass must be like this.

The Bread and Cup are raised and once again
The Resurrection happens, we are there
Walking on Easter morning with Christ's pain
Still crying from the Cross and in our ears.
Listen, the meaning's plain

All metaphors from music or from verse,
All purpose undiminished and fulfilled
All these occur in every form at Mass,
The Crosses stand there and today they yield
To all of us the grace

We need but may not name. Psalm after Psalm,
Passages from the Bible sing their way
Into our hearts and we are all made calm.
The Eucharist appears each hour of day
Through violence, alarm

And all the dark happenings of history.
We beat our breasts, cover our eyes and may
Weep a little. Sin is washed away,
All of Redemption each Mass will set free
The large Grace we must say.

All Saints 2000

They are anywhere but you won't find
Them easily. They are elusive and
Often shy. Some have a marvellous mind,
Others seem eccentric. They won't stand
In riches. They are kind

In ways not obvious. Wherever there
Is anguish of the flesh or mind or heart
Their presence can be sensed. They always bear
With the awkward who can play no part
In this world. They share

Strengths with Gandhi, the Dalai Lama. See
How Christlike are their manners. How exact
Their wisdom. They are haunters who set free
Those they harry. Sometimes they are racked,
Often they will be

With children, fools, the difficult. Some have
Special powers but none is a magician.
When others laugh they often will be grave,
So various, they share a great tradition
Which is bound up with love.

You may find one saint talking in a bar
And sharing jokes and views. Extravagant
They never are except in what they bear,
Lovable, a kind of element
Also, sometimes a star.

All Souls

Yesterday the holy ones by name
Were all remembered. We were edified
Yet also sweet affection rang their fame
They have set us standards which we've tried
To emulate. Today

All the holy, unnamed souls are called
To mind and heart. How they domesticate
Our otherwise more lofty thoughts. We're filled
With kindness, warmth. This is a crowded date,
November the second stilled

For a little while as we reflect
In church or street or office or at home.
We think about our own ends and connect
Our souls with these now gone, but they yet come
To mind in any act

We interrupt with our small contemplation,
We think of everlastings for a while
And all these souls rise in imagination
They are within a spiritual exile.
There is deep dedication

For all believers, those who ever dared
To credit what we all so dearly want,
A never-ending, but we're not prepared
For death. Words come to us, seem Heaven-sent,
A future life unfeared.

Song in November 2000

Count within me your minutes, hours,
    The turned tide of the sea,
Count me among your Summer flowers
    And Winter's leaf-bare tree.
Count me by every bell which rings,
    By every clock which ticks.
Count me in all your time-bound things
    And candles' blackened wicks.

Whatever loss still hurts for you
    Shed tears until your grief
Ends the story that is true,
    The pattern of your life.
Even if love should end you must
    Let it and be free.
Time blows away our fickle dust
    But, in arched memory,

Story by story still are told
    And no one tires of these,
They change to myths when they are old
    And show the shape of peace.
Count every death as ended war
    Which has its minstrelsy,
If you have ever loved before,
    Your book of memory

Shows page on page which you may turn
    And read or let alone
Doing either you can learn
    That birth and death are one.
We write the chapters of our lives
    By good or evil will
And page by page each one survives
    While someone reads them still.

Now is the turn of music to
    Choose trumpets, strings or drum.
They will assist each grief to go,
    Fresh happiness to come.
Music takes memory and lets
    Theme and use and range
Be heard in every note which fits
    And rings the needed change.

Turn the score of melody,
    Slowly let silence tell
The eager tale of memory
    That gives life yet stays still.

Carol for 2000

Put memory away. Today is new.
Carols and bells ring out and take the year
Into their power. They cast out pain and fear
    For everyone and you.

Put memory away. Soft sounds are rocking
A newborn child laid in a cradle made
For animals to eat from. Grace is said.
    A child puts out a stocking.

Put memory away and watch a world
Grown almost still because a baby can
Convince us he is born as God and man.
    The world's no longer old.

Put memory away. Tonight is Now.
And new as children's hopes and old men's eyes
Soon Kings will come and they are rich and wise
    But to a Child will bow.

Put memory away and have no fear.
A star is shining on a joyful sight.
A young girl's Child is born to us tonight
    And casts out pain and war.

New Year Song

This is the little space between
The marvellous birth and next New Year.
We've prayed and rid ourselves of sin
But still we feel the edge of fear.
So soon now we again begin

A year, a month, a way of life.
Three eager Kings are on their way.
A little child's been born in strife
But it is peace he brings to us
And gives our world another day,

Another year to mend our ways
And build our broken world again.
At Christmas we learn how to praise,
A little child fills all new days,
Forgiving sin, relieving pain.

Epiphany 2001

Three Kings or Three Wise Men – it is their day,
Their feast and with it we say our good-bye
To the new baby and the Christmas tree,
The gifts, the food but, most of all, the way
Light shone. It was an arrogant display.

The Kings bring gifts – gold, frankincense and myrrh,
The precious ore, the sweet scents we can share.
Outside today, the sun was everywhere
Yet sadness rises until, suddenly,
My father, I recall, was born today.

The melancholy goes for I recall
His sturdy mind, his to-and-fro of wits.
He thought that learning mattered for us all
And, what is more, gave me the taste for it
And hung such riches on my own mind's wall.

The Kings have come and gone. Epiphany
Moves to its close but now it leaves behind
A glow of Winter sunset in the sky.
Cards and gifts still throng my room and I
Can't bear to move them. Now my heart and mind

Rejoice together. Childhood comes back with
Its ripe regrets while age lights candles still
Partly to ease the eyes. O but their breath
Brings frankincense and myrrh and now they fill
Imagination. That small baby will

Guide us to Easter. Now I stand to pray
By a small crib and see the Child-God who
Waits for the world to say his words are true.
We can hoard now another Christmas Day
As Kings depart but by another way.

Night Song

Child in the womb or at breast,
Lovers at last at rest.
By the hands of the moon and sun
God's work is done.

This is the deep night.
The freezing winter light
Of stars gathers us all
Into God's call.

In and above all things,
He is the night-bird's wings.
We come to him at last,
Some slow, some fast.

Whitsun

It's Whitsun in a day or two and I
Think of the tongues of fire, the Holy Ghost
Brooding and teaching men the way to die
And never to feel lost.

A Holy time indeed but weather wears
A different look. It's grey but, nonetheless
A few birds' songs are audible. My verse
Has come back. Happiness

Is how I write and I know God is near.
Tongues of fire bear poetry to its height,
While holy rhythms take my words to where
There never is a night.

Hope

It is never gone for long.
It travels in dark caves and washes round
Slimy rocks but then it is out and off
Moving over wet ground:
This is the Sea of Hope which is sometimes rough,
Sometimes brief as a song,

When the tide of hope is out
The sun glitters above in a huge round
And the waves are dappled with light and you have no doubt
That here you are meant to be
For the Sea of Hope is your sea.

But not always yours.
This sea has moods as well as its bouyant tides,
Waves rising like horses, their great sides
Flashing with emerald
You are somewhere near
But not by this sea. It is true it reaches your ears
This sea in its many moods is also old,
Almost as old as time.

Stay not too far away
And wait for hope to return like a bold day
At Summer's glittering height,
Practise your fresh sight
And use it to compass the wide sea and land
There is such golden sound
And on the breeze words whisper to you
In psalms and song, all of them telling a true

Tale which you'll later turn to your own words
And your own work of rhyme
As the Sea of Hope comes in and the sky glows
And words are ready to choose
And this moment is their time.

Eden

There are moments when we find we are
Back in Eden. Its authentic air
Carries the breeze and draws up every flower
Sunwards and shining. Trees surround us but
Always a special one is heavier
With fruit and promise too. No gates are shut

But all swing to our touch. We do not go
Directly to one tree but back in sun,
Sit down a moment, then walk to and fro
Shaped of admiration, looking on,
Not picking anything. We do not know
What we've decided yet. All suns have shone,

The rising and the going. We don't choose
Consciously the moment when we shall
Gaze up at fruit and feel dry for its juice.
On we go, down trodden avenues
Until we pause at last, and then the fall
Happens. Sky grows darker and we lose

All sense of ease and leisure. Something is
Wrong at the heart of us. The sky reflects
Our mood. Clouds gather. There's a wilderness
Where order ruled each hour. We notice weeds,
We gaze towards the city and each mind collects
Round sudden ruins wrought by our misdeeds.

Perfection

Most dream of a perfected, holy thing,
A place or state. It's natural to our race.
The spur is not ambition. No, we bring
To this thought of ideals, a sense of grace.

Not grace itself for that is always earned
But a foreshadowing of how it can
Lead us to a place where many learned
About a real but insubstantial plan.

Matter never satisfies for long,
Power dwindles fast and leaves us wondering
Why we pursued it. In the soul a strong

Yearning for a personal truth will bring
Us to our knees and keep us there for long
And we won't shun all kinds of suffering.

Assurance Beyond Midnight

Wisdom or music come in these small hours,
Their clarities combine and I allow
Myself almost to rest in their good powers.

But it's a lively rest that I know now,
Compulsions cease and everything around
Fits in a meaning though I don't know how.

I only know rich purpose with a sound
Of settlements suggests itself and I
Listen for theme and arguments, the ground

Of God's great Being. Stars are very high
The moon is full, a warm September makes
Seasons a mood here though I don't know why.

But I know well that now my spirit wakes
And is assured. Imagination is
Rich. Helped out of sickness and heartbreaks

I feel in touch with everything that's peace
And later on there will arrive with dawn
A bold assurance and a synthesis

Of what waits for me not much further on.
But near enough to tell me faith is bold
And proves itself in all that has been done

To me and for me in a golden world.